Self-Portrait as Mostly Light

By

CL Bledsoe

Poems in this manuscript appeared in similar forms in the following journals:

Alan Squire Publishing Bulletin, Alien Buddha, Arkana, Arkansas Review, Bangalore Review, Barrow Street, BigCityLit, Bourgeon, Broadkill Review, Coachella Review, Delta Poetry Review, Eunoia Review, Feral: A Journal of Poetry and Art, Fowl Feathered Review, Gargoyle, Gyroscope Review, Hobo Camp Review, Journal of the Virginia Writers Club, Juke Joint, Maryland Literary Review, Mid-Atlantic Review, NoVA Bards, One Art Poetry Journal, Otherwise Engaged Literature and Arts Journal, Outcast Press, Panoplyzine, Poem Alone, Red Ogre Review, Rye Whiskey Review, Thimble, The Writing Disorder

"Barley and Vegetable Soup," won the 2022 Golden Nib regional award from the Virginia Writer's Club and placed third on the state level.

"I Wish You Were Fun" was nominated for a Pushcart Prize by One Art Poetry Journal.

The title "Self-Portrait as Mostly Light" is on loan from Michael Sikkema.

Contents

Duran Duran

Had I been raised by wolves,
wouldn't I have learned to hold
my liquor better than the moon

holds your eyes? We sharpened
our teeth on the lintel beams to
try to reach your light. We taught

our fleas to recite their mothers'
names in Latin. All to impress.
We were not wolves.

We were bears, fat and indolent,
too much milk and honey to ever
fit in that prom dress again.

That was the best night of my life,
Drunk on a thimbleful of hope.
White man dancing to the Cure.

Fur hidden beneath pink chiffon.
Everyone should be beautiful
at least once. Outside, the wolves

sang barbershop, with their slicked
back hair, their daddy's clean trucks.
They called us all cowards for leaving

the woods. I turned to stumble out
your name, but you were halfway
to the door, eyes full and gone.

I Wish You Were Fun

after a song by Sparks

I don't know what the birds are singing
about, but I suspect it's something to do
with their sciatica. Mirrors begrudge us
for not being Picassos. All sadness and past
due bills while needing a haircut. I wish
I was fun. I wish fear didn't strangle my smile
while I'm just trying to get the shopping
done. There's so much weight on my
shoulders, I can't look up. Laugh. At least
I'm not Ayn Rand. It's a different kind
of fear, that I can't open enough
to the world or that I can't close fast
enough. Either way, no one is happy
with every new recipe. So many times
it's about flirting with the void when all
you want is to be held by the darkness.
When I close my eyes and think of you
I see commercials. I'm sorry you aren't
happy, but I'm not going to be your midlife
crisis. The difference between an adventure
and a mistake is in the telling. These days,
I'm all mistake. Coward cowering indoors
for fear of storm. I'm already wet, and I have
so far to go in these squeaky shoes. But you
remember when I was fun. Were there ever
days before these?

Love Is Better Than a Warm Trombone

after a song by Gomez

Say, there are flowers by the door. A nervous
bee tugging on its bowtie. The neighbors have
pulled up chairs. Say, a box of childhood trauma,

a list of broken hearts, a warm trombone
tucked under arm. I was a movie star in LA.
Why haven't you heard of me? I was your mother's

favorite son. Every woman I meet either walks
the other way or asks me to move in. No one
wants to just go for sandwiches at that new place

downtown. Pickles and three kinds of cheese.
Mayo, an abomination before God. Please don't let
this be another fine example of American

miserableism. I've swallowed so much dirt,
I made it my bones. That's why I squelch when
I start to sweat. I don't mean to say anything

to make anyone uncomfortable. Nakedness
is more of a state of mind than an actionable offense.
I'll give you some of my honey so you can always

be my queen. The first name on the list is my own.

Don't Fuck It Up

Your eyes, a green I envy, their lushness
quiets me, warm waters in a moonlit night.
Peace tastes like honey on the tongue, salty
and sweet. I need you to understand how

I see you. I'm used to being small. You're used
to being strong. You are kinder than I could
ever be to myself. Let me be kind to you.

Where are you now? The noise
of the world can never shout down your
shameless smile. I will drive a hundred

miles to sit on your couch and watch murder
shows while you panic about how easy
this is. Let's lie in the grass for a little while

until our sneezing disturbs the squirrels.
Sweetheart, there will always be someone dying
in another room while you're trying to get
the laundry done. We can hire someone

to dust the bookshelves.

All the Doors Thrown Open

When the bombs come, we'll be happy ghosts
hiding from the giant spiders, our bodies no longer

aching from bad wiring, that thing we thought
was a good idea that one time and took months

to recover from. When the world becomes translucent
glass, outshining the jealous stars, and we finally feel

how substantial shadows are from the inside out,
dogs will bark at the smell of our souls, cats will beg

us for food our thumbs can no longer open. We'll fade
in the light and deepen under the moon, who will now

know our true names but still won't take our calls.
We'll no longer have hands to hold, my smoke entwined

in your smoke, nothing left but our curiosity. When
the world dies behind us, I'll remember the taste

of your mouth when you kiss me, the warmth
of your body held in my arms after long absence,

the sound of your laugh when you hear me mispronounce
words I've only read, the smell of your hair when

my face presses close, your eyes so bright when you're in love
with the world they remind me of what it is to be alive.

Coming Home

My brother's wife says we should be able
to choose not to put the feeding tube in.
I remind her of how he and I would argue,

when I was a teenager in the rice fields, about
my mother's last days. When my brother's
body clenches into itself, she says, that

should be the end. My mother, a pile
of awkward bones, twitching on the bed
when I'd come to visit, stayed with me

for years. I couldn't think of anything
to say. Does he moan like she did? Standing
at the door, screaming out over the pasture.

I used to hide in the bathroom, or coming home
from school, freeze at the bottom of the hill
when she was already screaming at the door.

She would say each of her children's names
in quick succession when one of us visited
the nursing home; one of them must be right.

My brother's wife assures me she could no
longer take care of him, though she tried. I
agree. I'll visit my mother's grave tomorrow.

Tell her I'm divorced now. My daughter
she never met. When I see my brother,
I'm worried most that I won't cry, that

he'll see in my eyes that I think he's already
dead, that all I'll be able to talk about
is the weather and the price of beans.

How To Dream the Delta

I'll start with mud and heat,
where all life begins.

I am a rice field, sweet flavor
in the air, a water moccasin
cutting across my surface,
a dancing cloud of mosquitoes
in my hair. My father is there,
mud thing, beer can tossed
in the back of the truck as he wades
out to patch a levee.

I am a black truck settling on a dirt track.
I am a snake rifle, pointing at myself.

My mother, a restless school teacher,
waits at the house. A little taste of hell
lit under her that spreads every day.
Tragedy is another name for home.

I am a red brick house on a ridge.
I am cows lowing in the yard since
the fence fell down.

My father comes home, thinks
he sees a skunk and shoots my dog.
My mother throws dictionaries at us
when we don't play school right.

I just want to have friends over
without worrying about the screaming.

There are wings somewhere far away.
Blackbirds we killed in our cornfields.
They are coming but never arrive.
You can hear them at night,
over the lonesome train. They will carry
me home when I'm ready.

Rice Farming

1

Muddy water and mosquitoes.
The sun burning just above your head.
My brother grumbled into the mud,
shovel on his shoulder with half-a-dozen
spills. He hesitated as much as you can
while walking through sucking Earth.
When he got to a spillway, he would lift
the plastic tarp carefully as snakes slithered
out across the brown levee. He'd make
a little cry at the surprise of them. Then it was
on to the next one.

2

My sister, when she was little, would go
with dad sometimes to the rice fields.
This day, she got tired of waiting
in the truck, got out to play with baby frogs
in the water until she got bored, put on
a grown-up's boots, and waded out
toward Dad. A few feet in, she got so
stuck, she couldn't lift her feet, just
as a water moccasin headed toward her.
She called out, "Dad!" He took two big
steps, swung his shovel, and cut
the snake in half. Then he lifted her
from the mud. "I told you to wait
in the truck," he said.

3

When Dad got home, he told my
brother he had a surprise in the back
of the truck. When my brother went
out, he found dead snakes, six or more,
shot with Dad's snake rifle that day
in the rice fields or in the ditches nearby.

Getting in the Cows

In my bedroom, I could hear them chewing,
a soft susurrus from the yard, scratching
their sides against the bricks of the house,
leaving tufts of hair. We had to round them up
in the fall, my uncles with cattle prods
they used more on us than the cows. Dad
with the glove pulled up to his shoulder.
The ground was rutted from hooves, mud
hardened until it was nearly unwalkable,
at the old barn we never used anymore,
which used to be where they made grape
and blackberry wine in an old bathtub.
The air was full of moos, cursing, men
doing work, rough hands in rough gloves.
I was always overwhelmed, I wanted
to play, to watch TV, to read. Anywhere
but here. The silage pit sat a few hundred
yards away, carved into the side of a hill
and covered with tarps. We'd try to climb
in, though they said we could get buried
and never be noisy again. It was something
to do other than get yelled at. We were
explorers looking for a way through to another
world, any other world.

When I Was Young

The days came thick, a soup like swampy air,
rife with buzzing moments. How will I divide

the hours into pure and forgotten? Whose lamp
should I follow through the toothed night?

Years of repeated questions before I asked
my own. Sadness passed from hand to hand,

savored and held sacred. So much of life
is about aching upward until the slow fall

and rest. If you narrow the eyes in anger,
you might not have to see as much of what you fear.

There were ghosts in the woods we played in.
A ghost in the bedroom, my mother's voice

fading with dawn. It's best to think of Sisyphus
happy, but what games did he play as a child?

They're thinner, now, the days, slow as snow
clotting the cool grass. I can see the soil

through them, now. It won't be much longer.

Worship

It's a kind of worship, love. The altar
of your body. The secret of yourself
you've shared with me. I am strong

enough to understand what it is
that makes you. That unmakes me.
This is what I've always wanted,

you. My life's work will be your unveiling.
The rebuilding of myself. Together.
When you smile, I feel as if I'm standing

in sunlight. The tight bun of your hair,
the blood of the universe. The blood
of the future being born. Life. Every day

with you is the best it's ever been. Like
in movies. That you care enough to yell.
That you take my hand. It's a calming fire,

love, which devours everything that was,
births all that will be. Not in penitence.
But in prayer.

Happy

Let's make the choice right now to be happy,
no matter where Epictetus' lamp might lead.
Stand still as long as you can, as the wind
blows detritus into your eyes, but despair
will find its way into your heart. Why not let
me in? I've been standing outside
your door so long, you hit me every time
you throw out the dishwater. I see you in my
dreams. In my life. As you are. We're all
broken. That's the price of playing. The only
way to win is to slip out the back while the bouncer
is distracted. I've been a kicked dog licking
strangers' hands. You've been a nameless
daughter. Let's learn the oboe and tour the south.
Whatever there is to say between us, let's spend
the rest of our lives working it out.

Learning How to Fall

after a song by Blonde Redhead

I will stay with you, like blackbirds settling
on a line, till it sags from comfortable use.
There will always be a smoother voice
but you know all the jokes I like. Bring your cold
feet to bed and warm them on my legs. Hope
is such a little thing, in the eyes, in the breath.
It barely dents the air, though it moves so fast.
So much of my life has been about shrinking
to fit in the frame, the dumbest flower
in captivity, pining for the rain. Darling, let's grow
together until we shadow the past. I know that ghosts
can walk through walls, but I'm learning
how to fall through the floor—whatever it takes
to get outside, where you are. Your eyes
are an elegy in the shape of a river. Your eyes
are the ghost of a tomorrow that finally came. Baby,
let's find the answers to the biggest mysteries
in the world, like how do we make these fat wings
fly? Why are we lingering when the body's gone cold?

Come Back

Come back. Even as a shadow, even as a dream.
-Euripides

I've always thought of darkness as warm,
the comfort of familiar pain. Most crimes
against me happened in the light. The reason
I'm happy to wake up is that you call me
in the mornings. My knee is still bleeding
and there are feathers in my tea bags. Eggshells
reforming in the sink disposal. To be a man
is to be afraid that a woman doesn't need you.
She doesn't. I can't stop thinking about
your face, lying back on the pillow, eyes
closed in ecstasy. I've never seen anyone
so beautiful. Love means remembering
that time you said you needed something,
and being it. Love is a way of listening.
These days, we take turns helping each
other put the dying and dead to rest and then
it's time for snacks. Let me rub your feet
while you doze on the couch. Let me hold
your body while neither of us speak. I need
it. When the shells sprout, I'll make you eggs.
Try not to think about where they came
from. We never leave anything behind,
no matter how fast we limp. Just let me kiss
you a little longer before you leave.
Then I'll go back to bed, but I won't sleep.

Go On, Love Me. It Does You Good.

From an ancient Greek inscription, author unknown

If there is a pit, there must be a sky. Air
bunches beneath fingers, washing cleaner
than dirt. Count every footstep until
you stumble, and then start over. In this
way, a life is made. My brain
stutters when I see you. Clichés slap me
in the face and steal my shoes. You die so
much brighter than the rest of us. Sitting
in the sun until the cats make you their queen.
Somewhere between a smirk and a supernova,
the obsidian soil in your eyes. Tell me
a story about bad choices. About the way wisdom
forgets its name when the sun hits just
right. I've been collecting thoughts
all my life for this very purpose. It's time.
All of this means so much. It has to.

The Mythology of Us

I will sing along with the song
of your smile for as long as you let
me. Darling, we're too old to be
this clever. The pricked ears of the world
wait, warmed in the darkest light.
You are the crack of thunder outside
my cave. The plains of Mars on my tongue.
Skin so soft my fingers ache to touch.
Hold me in your eyes. Is that wood smoke
ahead, the slowest winter day, furry
cat on the lap and nothing important
on TV, or is it the end? Don't let it be.
You can trust me. I'm not smart enough
to do anything but love you. I'm not afraid
of hard work. But let's make it easy. Don't
be afraid. All I want is to pull
you tighter. You fit so well in my arms.
What more do you need to know?

This is how it is with me:

I order the same meal every time
we go out because I was paying attention
to you instead of the menu. I have 54 tabs
open on my phone of things you've said
you might want to do. I started a notebook
of all the places I want to go
with you. My fridge is full of things
you might like to eat. I forgot
that thing you said one time because
I was listening to the sound of your voice.
I work all the time. Don't think
I'm neglecting anything important
on the phone with you all hours.
My love, when you come to bed in a tee-shirt,
turn away from me and show me your neck,
when you fall asleep on my shoulder
and I don't move for an hour, I've made
a place for you, feathered the sides of my
life, painted the sky, the aching red and green
of my soul. I watch your mouth, waiting
for the moment you'll move in close
and fill me with your desire.

I Only Feel Safe When It Rains

I launched my small life onto the dark side
of the moon, a beautiful parade of the same
day for years on end. Tycho Brahe couldn't

see me shivering amidst the constellations.
It's easy to appear strong to a mirror, reflecting
the familiar light. I sipped the milky sky

to grow strong, kept my head down and accepted

my place in the rotation. But it's so hard to be
your own dawn when none of the mornings left
in the world are taking reservations. You came

to my door in light, a sigh of beauty. Shattered
the midafternoon lull, verve to accent the horizon,
color painting the sky. How could someone

so vibrant live in the gray dust we've made

this place? Everything falls away in your eyes; my
life, a moldering crater. I want to burn in orbit
around you, fear peeling away to greet the dawn.

Barley and Vegetable Soup

Winter comes, and we're proud of ourselves
for eating soup in season. Lentils and split pea,
like our grandmothers, who always kept
their clothes from splitting in time.

When bad things happen, it's important
to remind ourselves that we're real, even
when we don't want to be. The same is true
of love and pumpkin pie, which no one likes

enough to eat more than once a year. Every day,
I could be happy waking to the soft susurrus
of your breath. The flash of your eyes. Only
a dying flame is brighter. I could make you

barley vegetable soup to remind you what it is
to be alive. It's not just that we're dying; it's
those winter mornings. The fire warming our feet.
The crows calling somewhere outside.

Dog in the Rain

I'm thinking about time, the slow
avalanche of insistence. The man
singing in the rain below my balcony
and the father you lost four months ago.

I'm thinking about the shape of your
heart, the wound he left, gouged bloody.
I've pushed against the edges, trying
to skirt the bruise but stay inside. I must

be quiet long enough for you to think,
to make space for yourself amidst your grief.
The man in the rain drags his dog from corpse
to corpse, birds, trash; cutting a curious shape

into the night. He seems happy, the way strangers
always seem happier for no reason other than
lack of familiarity. I close my eyes to see
your face, the sun you've burned through

my darkness. I've been given so much.
The man disappears into his apartment,
and I'm alone in the night air. A drink
on one side, empty chair beside me, waiting.

Date Night

On our movie date night, you snuck in bourbon,
collapsible cups, Coke, sparkling lemon water.
A woman down the row glared while we got
drunk on a passable superhero movie. Legs
entwined. I have to stop myself from touching
you every few seconds. Your lips, your eyes, so
beautiful my heart sputters like a man proved
wrong. I want you upside down in the back
of my eyes. I want to kiss your neck, your soft
skin against my lips, the smell of your hair. After,
we drank more at the arcade downstairs, played
broken games until we won enough to trade for
a gift for my daughter. You rode home with me,
too wasted to drive, and made scones with too
much sugar while we watched Christmas movies.
Once, you asked me what my happiest memories
were. It's you, that next morning, curled into my
chest. Your breasts and stomach while you were
getting dressed. The shape of your lips
when you say my name.

The Work of Dying

My sister says come now. I can't
afford it, but I do. Sleep on her
couch with her massive puppy whose love
is like a cyclone overwhelming a picnic.

My brother twitches in a hospital bed, unable
to turn himself without a nurse. It's excruciating,
the constant motion, his nerves dying cell
by cell. He is trying to climb a hill with no top.

His stomach aches all the time. The nurses
want him to eat on his own as long
as he's able. Autonomy is important for mood.
We bring sugary snacks, all of his favorites.

I go for extra ice, stand over him, bone thin,
and feed him snack cakes and water. He gums
them slowly, struggling to control his jaws.
I wait with the next bite. I can't speak.

We decorate his room, hang tinsel, a little
tree, photos where he can see them.
I'm here for two days. We stop by mom's
grave and polish the stone. On the way back

to my sister's house, I tell her I blame
myself for not being here. She can't stop crying.
It's like I've fallen over the railing, sleep-
walking, but I can't hit bottom.

Self-Portrait as Mostly Light

after a line by Michael Sikkema

Two fingers in the glass you gave me, not the good
stuff but the okay stuff just in case. A panic attack tamped
down as long as you don't call again. It's not about separating

the broken parts out like chaff; that morning in the hotel
is load-bearing trauma, the lies I wanted to believe spit
through your perfect teeth. Everything is terrible

and I can't stop missing you no matter how much
I hate myself. My heart closed tight as a fist shoved
into pocket, I throw back the glass and ignore the rug

you bought me, the shoes, the pile of unworn clothes by my bed.
It really ties the place together. The sky is heating up, finally.
I can sit on the balcony and watch the world come alive.

I am nodding off, trying to wake from the dream of you.

Clumsy

I've died here before. I've died here
and kept stumbling toward that place
where everyone is safe. I've seen it
on tee-shirts. I hear helicopters, but they
aren't for me. You were the only way
I could rise. Don't leave me with the moon
for my only friend. It's cold and they banned
me from Waffle House for starting
a fire. I miss you. The moon misses not being
the coldest place in town. Come back
and let me learn to love you the way you want
to be loved. I'll be all right. Take my arm
as we walk into oncoming traffic. The fuckers
will stop if we glare hard enough. I'll be
the bed you stumble toward, half-blind and drunk.
You've got your cat and wine but they won't keep
you warm. Baby, I've got a fireplace. I'll use
myself for kindling.

It's a Damp, Drizzly November in My Soul

You kissed like you regretted being seen, like
a chore. It's nothing special that you laughed
at my jokes; everyone does. Abuse makes
the tenderest meat. When you called to cry
about how lonely you are, I thought about work
the next day, about the plans I had for the weekend
without you, about how I wouldn't sleep
that night or maybe the next. "You didn't have
to be lonely, sweetheart," I said. "You don't get
to call me that anymore," you said. All weekend,
I sat in the rain and tried to feel cold. I'm sorry.
I'm sorry I believed you when you said that you
loved me. I'm sorry for whatever it was about
me that made you choose wine rather than me.
If you think you're the only one broken
by the world, you're as stupid as me.

A Burning in the Air

There were things I meant to say
about the struggle to take light in
hand. The longest travail of human
history has been where to find
water and how to take it with
us. Light's like that. It will be all
around except when we need it.
It's easy to forget the power of
darkness, the way it quiets the roar
of the world. There is a kind of catfish
in a cave in Kentucky that never
sees light. I've lived in houses
like that, full of eyeless complainers.
Light is so forbidding they gave it
names but couldn't make it love us.
If you look too closely into its
eyes, you lose yours. There are great
penalties for wanting to see things
more clearly. One has to wonder.

Dust

I can't get the taste of dust out of my mouth,
which is another way of saying I miss back
home, everyone scrabbling for the best tree
to be buried under. None of them have the knees
to climb anymore. It's different where you
grew up. Maybe red and soft like a hound's
fur. Maybe white as bone in the sun. I'm waiting
for love to see my text and remember that fine
is better than terrible. I am trying to be more. Here,
they buy it in bags. No one's dying from a lack
of rain. Someone I never thought about loving thought
I was famous, now that I'm away. I asked, wouldn't
you have heard of me then? Even the best zip
codes still have worms, though, all the hungrier
for lack of bodies. I couldn't stand under all that
shade so I came out into the sun, and now here
I am. The thing about dust is it comes with you,
wherever you go. In your cuffs. In your hair.
I can't sleep without a little bit of it in my bed.
A little taste of what I thought
I'd never miss until I heard it missed me.

Grimaldi the Clown

Grief makes for a shabby coat, which the chill
is fine with. The mistake, always, is wanting
to be warm. My ex used to hold me for long
minutes as soon as I walked into her townhouse.
Not speaking, the door, still open behind me,
her warmth filling my senses. I've never missed
someone so much. When you're crying
in your car on the way home from the comic
book store, pay attention to the light so you don't
get honked at. The other drivers have their own
grief to meet. I have so much to say,
and none of it matters to you. Are you still
unhappy? Or did all my good intentions take?
If it's a mixed drink, is it really day drinking?
No one can tell at work if you don't smile
too much. When the meeting's moved back,
it gives you time to sober up. Everything dies,
it just takes so fucking long. Have an apple
and a power bar and wait your turn.

Three Months

Shaking hands. Shaking body. A red licorice panic
twirling up my throat for days each time she calls.

Stay busy. Projects. Work, like a weighted blanket. Date
anyone, but be nice about it. Movies. Shows. Stand

outside friends' houses until they get home. Don't
make it weird. Bring dinner. Flowers. Be on.

Be fun. Be everything they want. Be not alone
until it passes. Alcohol is expensive and food sobers, so

not eating is just being fiscally responsible.
When she texts, tell her that you miss her, but not

right away, because she won't text back. Don't
tell her that your ship broke against her shore. Tell her

that you'll try harder to need less. When friends
say you should block her, tell them that you're fine.

Smile. Tell a joke about mushrooms. Don't remember
the times she made you feel like no one could ever

want you. So many times. It's true. She doesn't. She
never did. This isn't real life. These things happen

in movies. How could you be so pathetic. Thinking
means realizing each thing she said that wasn't true.

Each time she blamed you for being hurt. She was never
sober with you. She used you like a crutch and you

were just happy to be there. And you would take
her back. No, you wouldn't. But you're not so sure.

Burr

Cooking pork steaks in the kitchen
in your underwear, while the grease
popped on your big belly. You'd eat them
flat on your back with a plate on your
chest. I never understood it. In many ways,
my father. The only one who listened
to my jokes. You used to carry us around
on your shoulders. Took us trick-or-treating
down the hill. Drove me to concerts
of your favorite bands and quizzed me
on them in the car. When I got older,
I used to call and tell you all my troubles,
before I realized I didn't have any yet.
I want to hear your voice, replaying
your favorite TV show of the last
week in detail, and how it reminded you
of another show I'd like, which you'd then
launch into. You taught me how to tell
stories. Brother, you gave me your time
and attention, which is what a father
should do. I had to get away, go fail
somewhere else with less sun and fewer
mosquitoes. Before the imposter
became a syndrome. That time when
I brought my daughter to visit,
you were so thin. Barely able to walk.

My Brother

A giant bed.
A giant man, lying.
A plate on his chest.
Life to be devoured.
Record player bumping across the house.
60s jam bands. Live albums.
8-tracks stacked on a bookshelf.
Cheap westerns. Destroyer novels.
Richard Pryor. Redd Foxx.
The smell of stale rot.
No woman has ever been in there.
A bathroom we never use.
Band posters on the wall, The Guess Who.
Mountain on the stereo.
My brother, pontificating about each band.
Listen to this solo.
He wanted to be a drummer,
but never learned to play.
A ping-pong table, replaced by a spare bed.
We used to chase each other with his dirty socks.
He managed the fish shop in the winters,
worked long hours driving a combine,
cutting levees in the rice fields
with me and my father.
The sun, a constant weight.
Man made from mud returning to mud.
Me, complaining.
Me, lecturing the air.
Me, so young and unloved.
Him, listening.

Burr Dream

On the night of my dead brother's birthday,
I dream his body has grown feet from his
belly. A ring of them, some protruding whole,
others a nub or somewhere in between.
They're hidden under his shirt, and it's only
when he's home at the end of a hard day
in the fields that he frees them. It's a gift
to me, to see his true self. They exist
to let him run faster than he ever could away
from the niggling uncle, the negligent father.
He is a man belittled daily, left to read
his westerns and dream of being the lone
hero with a gun riding down the outlaws.
The rock star cheered on by fans.

In the dream, he was heavy again, not
the blanched 155-pound body he was
at the end. You couldn't see the shape
of his bones or fingernails long with neglect.
Hale and whole, rice fields
behind him and something good on TV.

This Is the Classic Story

after a line by Eleni Sikelianos

A card table in the back room
of the Fish Shack where my brother
always tried to find the trick;
if he could beat the house, he could find
that piece that never fell into place
for him. Still living in our parents' house,
he listened to music voraciously,
teasing out solos and quizzing
me so we could find the trick
together. He took me to my first
concerts, and we listened,
eyes askance, silently interpreting.
He worked as the manager at the Fish
Shack, fileting catfish or buffalo fish
however you wanted. Customers
could pick greens from our uncle's
garden while they waited. My brother
cut fish with his head in the sky. He
was working on a mystery, listening
to a song no one else could hear.

Pecans

Pecan tree in the side yard, another
by the carport. We used to climb
its double trunks to the lowest
branches. Up there, it was Oz,
Narnia, Hollywood, and everything
else. My sister's cat chased
my dumb dog up it after it kept trying
to eat her food. We waited for fall for the green
nuts to ripen. We'd gather them, grumbly-
mouthed, in big trash bags and distribute
them to friends, the leftovers dumped
in the deep freeze, now that mom
was too sick to cook. I struggled
to get to those higher branches
until I was finally tall enough, then
I was too heavy.
There were tree ants. An introduction to bugdom
on its trunk. A bird nest in its branches.
I would sit long hours, reading, waiting
for dad to come home, listening
to the world carrying on down the hill.

Mother's Day

1

I remind my daughter to
make her mother a card
for Mother's Day. Something
nice, I say, make it when
you're not mad at her.

2

To be a good father you must bleed
a trail from silence to work ethic,
something to scrawl on the divorce papers
in place of your name. Everyone has
some great advice that's never touched air.

3

My father spent his long days
drinking to escape his forgotten life.
Eyes always cast out over the waters
of tomorrow, he never had anything
to say even about the weather.

4

After her divorce, my mother stayed
to convalesce at my father's house.
As she drifted further from home in
her mind, she sat for long hours, staring
out the window, just past the television.

5
"I wonder if I'll get anything for my
birthday this year," I say while driving
my daughter back to her mother's.
My daughter stares out the window
at something I've forgotten how to see.

Butterflies

And maybe it's all the same, the butterflies
she's scared of because you can't trust
beauty, the bees with their honey, the night.
Ants are more honest, watching the tire
swing but not daring climb aboard.
She's getting too old for wonder. That's
what they say. Time to nod off in math class
and hope for the best after college.
The wind is just another way to be lonely,
sunlight sonorous on her face. You can hear
it melting our dreams. We did it to ourselves,
I guess. No, we did it to them. No, it wasn't
us. They have names and addresses.
But the butterflies come from far and wide,
looking for flowers, looking for eyes
to watch them flutter away.

Fly Around My Pretty Lil Miss,

after the traditional song

My daisy. My honey. My pretty
lil miss. Sundresses and hairclips.
Scooting across the carpet, too
curious to crawl. It was me
and you playing on the floor,
while people did whoknows
around us, or at the zoo where
everyone recognized us because
we went so much. That picture
where a chimp is watching you,
oblivious. Vomit on my shirt
and joy in your eyes. The days
move so fast. Now, it's every other
weekend and one day a week
for dinner. Lucky to have that.
Love can make life harder. But
I wouldn't sacrifice my time
with you for something easier
to stand. Fly around, my honey.
If I had my pretty little girl,
I'd feed her sugary candy.

I'm Gonna Be an Engineer

after a song by Peggy Seegar

My daughter demands choices.
She doesn't want to wear a skirt, or
maybe she does today.
She doesn't want to wear makeup, or
maybe she does today.
She says she's like Frida, she doesn't pluck
her eyebrows. If someone doesn't
like it, that's their choice.
She wants to be a principal at a school.
She wants to adopt a kid.
She wants to travel the world
and write about it.
I used to try to make her want
to be an engineer. I bought kits
for us to build together. But she'd
rather work with animals.
She's waiting on her first kiss.
She's more concerned with her friends.
She doesn't have to be an engineer,
but she can if she wants to.

Wonderful Time

I've had a wonderful time, but this wasn't it.
-Groucho Marx

Somebody call the National Guard because this
heart's about to overthrow the status quo.

I need a garlic press for my disappointment,
to find the perfect lovely clove of hurt.

I'm making a delicious soup from crocodile tears
and tail. To serve to your estranged mother who likes
me best.

I've got a new warehouse to burn, a vacant lot
to rebuild into million-dollar condos. As soon as
I get my sleep right and my PTSD alphabetized.

Baby, you can't afford to live in me on your
professor's salary. You better learn to do math.

McDonald's French Fries

Our Christmas date was to see the Nutcracker
at the Kennedy Center. You got drunk,
like every time we went out, and on

the way home, we stopped at McDonald's
so you could get three large fries. A secret
I'm no longer keeping. You ate them on

my couch while I rubbed your feet, afraid
to ask why you were so sad when we'd had
such a nice night. Maybe because you missed

your dad. Maybe because you were with me. I've
decided to be angry instead of missing you, to
wipe you from my sleeves like dipped-in milk.

Grief is such a feeble thing. Fragile as a crack.
Thin as spun glass. It mumbles, forcing the ears
to prick. It places its hand on your shoulder

when you try to run. My brother died a few days
after you left me. I was still drunk from you
and couldn't cry due to my meds. He told

the nurse he was ready to go home to Jesus
and they found him dead a little while later.
I can't help but envy his ease in letting go.

I told myself I should be grieving one or
the other, I should be fixing whatever you hated
in me, I should be kicking clear of that night

when it seemed like things were finally turning
around. I never liked McDonald's fries. I wouldn't
have even watched the Nutcracker without you.

My brother, my dear brother, will stay with me
when you've drunk your last bitter days through.

Late-Stage Brunch

Half the people are afraid the world
is changing. The rest of us are afraid
it won't. The days fail so spectacularly
someone should be taking pictures.
If you're looking for a partner to get
serious about procrastination, I'll get
back to you on my availability. Open
the windows to let the birdsong in.
Plot murder on the neighbor who always
gets hummingbirds. An eruption
of squirrels whenever I toss something
in the dumpster. Happiness on a horizon
that forever moves forward. Eventually,
you've got to stop chasing it. Sit and admire
the way it lights up the distant sky.
Have a scone with your tea and don't
think about who you'd rather share it with.

Melody of Certain Damaged Lemons

after a song by Blonde Redhead

I turtled my days, a wince of light.
You come to my bed every night.
Your bloodshot eyes won't remember
my number for long, or maybe I'm wrong.
Maybe the end will come in flames and no one
will be left to complain about how hard
it is to push air through stiff lips when all
anyone wants is to be a capybara with a never-
ending supply of lemon cheesecake. Can't you see
that I'm dying? Your love
is like the knife scarring the tree; everyone
can see your name on me. That used to be
enough until I sobered up. But I'm not sober.
I'm your only friend, and that hurts worst of all.
I blocked your number, and I'm waiting
for you to call and tell me you saw.
The trees are muttering complaints. The wind
is unhappy with its wardrobe. So much matters
to those who don't care at all. Everything
that you touch breaks. I wanted
to be your hands. I wanted to be the shards
on the floor.

After a Line by Tina Chang

I'm haunted by how much my mother
never knew about my life. Pretty school
teacher who married a shiftless farmer. She
read romance novels and left
her husband every couple of years. But he
always talked her back. He clung to her,
his lifeboat in the stormy seas of whiskey.
Maybe that's why she stayed; she couldn't
bear to not watch him sink the last time.
For me, it was sadness, which is so much less
sexy. I tried to take whatever
was in front of me without watching
the horizon too much. So much of myself defined
by chemicals and bad advice. Why stay alive?
Was always my problem. Why engage and for
what gain? So much time to have been enjoyed
if only I could.

Thick Socks

I didn't know it was raining until I went
to water the pansies, just that I needed

a hoodie and thick socks as soon as I got
out of bed. It's so cold without you here.

But once the socks are on, there's no

going out today. I don't make the rules.
Who among us hasn't felt like an uninvited

guest in our own lives? The story goes that
Charlie Chaplin once came in twentieth

in a Charlie Chaplin lookalike contest.

He probably did a lot better than I
would've, since I don't even own a top hat.

Another failing. I miss you. I miss the way living
makes sense when you're with me. It's not a thin

thing, hope; it's watered on milk and honey, rode

the elevator in its descent to miffeddom. It came
for the local jellies. The squirrel juggling

championship. It will dissipate with the sunset
but be out early for that McDonald's senior

citizen discount coffee. I open the door

to the wind, trudge to the store in the rain. Get
that bread you like so it's like you might make

a sandwich at any moment. I'll keep the fancy
mustard handy. Just come back. Hurry.

You and Me

There are two kinds of lovers, the broken and the young,
both are doomed but reborn in each other's eyes. A lawyer

and a doctor walk into a bar. One argues for the truth
of the heart, the other cuts away the disease that eats it.

Both will be stuck with the tab at the end of the night.
I've been the lawyer, so sure that I can argue down

disdain; the doctor, trying to heal the broken at all costs.
Nobody wants to drink alone, but everyone does.

I no longer go to bars; I've moved them into my living
room, late evenings spent dazed and missing she-who-

will-not-be-named. Once the fruit had been eaten, Eve begged
the snake to say her name just once more. Through the blinds,

I watched the life I've always wanted step into a waiting car,
a hint of leg through that red dress. There's nothing so pedestrian

as feeling things deeply. Maybe it was when I was on the way
to the store, maybe it was eavesdropping on the true language

of the moon, but I was safe in my world of pain
when you arrived in shadow, a doctor I could heal,

a lawyer I could convince. There are two kinds of lovers,
you and me. We'll take turns buying each other drinks.

I've got space on my patio, some jazz drifting
over the slow night. In the parking lot, all the lives

we never wanted take turns crashing into each other
while we sip.

Someplace Soft

Every one of us is looking for someplace soft
and warm to die, I want it to be in your eyes,
the dark quiet. Just hold me a little while
so I don't have to think about what to do.

You've got this fire I want to get up next to
and say sweet things. Baby, every word out
of your mouth is a cool drink of water after
shoveling mud all morning. Your voice

is home. I don't feel alone no more now
that I know you're in the world. Pretty girl
they're only lies if we don't make 'em true.
You can be my sun if you want, and I'll be

yours too. There's a line of bodies trailing
behind each of us, all of them forgetting
their own names but whispering that pain
that keeps them here. Let's set it down.

There's a whole lot of nothing to do out there.

You're Tougher Than a Bump of Raw Medicine

from a line by De La Soul

A ghost whose tie will never lie right.
A ghost with see-through teeth hoping to impress.
I'm trying to master the secret language
that only we speak, the language
of our bodies. You are a beautiful dream
I never want to wake from.

Four hours pass between glances.
Four hours pass and I can't step away
from your voice. I need it like caffeine
in the morning, like the plans that keep
me hoping: this time. Let me soak in the warmth
from your smile and never know fear again.

Baby, you're like the sunset after a hard
day, let me hold your face in my hands
until I grow solid. Let's load up my battered
car, travel the country solving crimes. Let's
climb the mountain of everything that's fallen
away to lead us to these days. Let's be happy,
baby we deserve it. It's so close, I can see
it in your eyes.

My Sister's Grief

Is a full glass on wobbly legs,
hovering over a laptop she can't
afford to replace.

Is a phone call to make sure
I'm not driving after my second
drink.

Is a fast thing, red and darting,
whereas mine is slow and well-fed.

Rides quietly beside her but mumbles
just out of hearing when she's trying
to get home from work.

Is a card in the mail, left on the table
to be opened.

Is a ringing phone that might be work.

Sits with her when she finally has time
to eat but doesn't speak.

Asks her how her day has been and talks
over the answer.

Settles in while she's making dinner. It has
stories to tell, but remembers them all wrong.

Reminds her after the sun brightens
the morning: I am here.

I'm Never Going to Know You Now

from a line by Elliott Smith

You were young and bright, heart
full of butterflies, long walks
in the evening. A new boy at the movies
every Friday night. All grown, you tried.
What a disappointment life can be.
You opened your heart to the world.
It forsook you, like a bad boyfriend.
But you kept going to his house, as if
this time, it would be different.
You didn't have a choice. I was all noise
and runny nose, bored in front of the TV.
You were ice cream with onions. A walker
that didn't help. I would scream in your face
and run and lock myself in the bathroom.
I didn't have a choice. Now, you'll never
know me. Single dad to a beautiful
daughter who looks just like you.
I don't have your disease, so neither
will she. You might've liked me,
if you'd had the chance.

My Sister Describes Cooking with Our Mom.

It was her job to put the lettuce and other
veggies in a big pot of cold saltwater.

"We have to get all the bugs off," Mom
would say. A school teacher and farm

wife, she knew where things came from,
that the detritus of the past had to be washed

free. My sister stole her best silver spoons
to dig a swimming pool in the front yard.

She was going to line it with trash bags.
Mom used to pay her a quarter to do chores.

Once, when no one else was home,
my sister got me to help move all the furniture

out of Mom and Dad's room and switch
it with hers. When they returned, she refused

to switch it back. In the kitchen, frog legs
frying in an electric skillet for Dad.

My sister would eat pancakes with no syrup,
fried bologna with mustard sandwiches,

tuna salad, potted meat sandwiches. Helping mom
bake her birthday cake. All of this was when

my sister was little. By the fourth grade, mom
was too sick to cook much anymore. My

memories are fragmentary at best. I rarely cook,
myself.

Nursing Homes

I got ads for nursing homes after
you told me your plan to save Dad
from one. A reverse mortgage on
his house, his land as collateral
for a loan. Capitalism thinks
he's lived too long. Nowhere
is safe from the marketers. I steal
a horse, learn to ride it, and bump
up to the tallest Arby's I can find.
Heavenly roast beef, marinating
in milk and honey. That's what
they say on TV. A man follows
me in asking about my horse's
warranty. Sure, most of them died
as babies, but weren't the prehistoric
men happier without Capitalism?
No neighbors playing loud music
on worknights. My father
used to hop a train and ride into
Memphis for the day, RC Cola
and Moon Pies for a nickel. So much
has changed for the better.
But it sure doesn't feel that way.

Diogenes, Holding Up Your Heart: Behold, Love

All my life, I've been trying to save my mother,
who died so badly. Ten years old, mixing
tuna in a bowl with mayo, chopped up pickles.

I sat with her when everyone else was out,
watching TV while she muttered
and screamed about the pain of her nerves, dying.

Will she ever be saved? If I fix some broken
lover, will the ghost's cries outside my door
fade? Or will I simply move on to the next?

Most mornings at work, I cross the river,
scorpion on my back, imagining a world
that doesn't drown. The shore, so near.

After your father died, you called me still drunk
and said this was our first date, the four-hour call,
the Zamboni of grief smoothing off your heart.

I wish I were a saint, so you could burn me
for warmth, crucify my grief as salvation
for your own. I could let you drown us both.

But I was never a thief to be taken to heaven,
a friend to birds or travelers. I wanted to love
you, to be happy at your side, stupid frog that I was.

Wasp Honey

The first rule in life is you're going to get stung.
The question is whether you get the honey.
You'll be standing there, like a fool, regardless
of how much you meant it. The wasps meant
it too. Name anything that isn't a metaphor
for love. Don't say love, because none of us
will admit we believe in that. But we hope.
She said she'd been smiling all week
when I told her how beautiful she looked
last night. I didn't tell her I started drinking again
because it was the only way I could stay
alive. The problem with the past is it won't
go away just because it's over. You have to dig
a hole in the desert, beat it to death
with the shovel, and kick the past in, still screaming.
If I could see you, I'd say don't call my name,
no matter how much I want to hear it.

Please Remember Me, My Misery, and How It Lost Me All I Wanted

after a line by Iron and Wine

I can hear my miseries muttering in the other room
while I watch the floor refuse to move. They
think there's something wrong with me that isn't
them. It's embarrassing. They make excuses
to sneak out. When the smoke clears from
the dirty oven, I will tell you a secret no one else
knows. It has something to do with the proper
baking temperature of root vegetables, specifically
rutabagas. When it rains, be careful with the morning
or else it might fall apart like drenched paper. Sometimes,
you've got to just watch things until they firm up.
This is pretty close to a universal truth, except
it was never translated to Latin. Many things predate
the smell of her hair, the taste of her sweat.
Soup. The memory of absence. The tedium of despair.
It will only get worse. Someone will regret you
the way you regret her. Someone will taste your
neck and feel at home while you look only
backward. The real truth is that the more deeply
someone gets to know you, the less they'll like
you. This includes yourself.

Self-Portrait as Mostly Light 2

after a line by Michael Sikkema

Black is slimming, so I ate two nights
and let them swirl in my veins until
I couldn't see you anymore. A little
something for the stomach, a little
something to help me sleep. You can
only keep busy for so long, hoping
death will claim you before you have
to sit still and remember what you've
done. I need a haircut. I need to drop
fifty pounds. I need to hear you say
you're sorry. The sky is so bright,
I want to go for latkes at that truck
by where I used to work. I was thin
and miserable in a different way.
Waiting for the world to open its ears

Again, Again, Again

In these waning hours, I'm searching
for the one who wants to buy and sell
me, if only a better economy. The one
who is multitude, all named beige.
But it goes with anything! The one
who'll sell my secrets to the Russians
as soon as they mail a check. It's my own
fault. I've placed my name in so many
hats, none of which would fit without
looking a little silly. But I don't mind.
The outstretched hands all twisting
at the wrist, dropping the slip of paper
at first or fifth glance. Perhaps
I need to adopt a harsher accent when
whispering my own name to the cosmos.
Perhaps the mistake is ever intending it
to be heard. I smiled at seven sunsets
and tried to make them dawns. I waited
all day to do it. I burned the photographs
of seven seekers who no longer wanted to
be seen. I don't want any trouble. Let's
all be reasonable. The problem with intent
is thinking it's yours.

Bear

I ate bear until I became bear. Digested
by crows and shunned by the rich.
Berries and salmon for breakfast.
The slower friend for lunch. Nothing
is the way they told us it would be,
and yet we blame ourselves.
I wandered the mountains until I found
a man lonely enough to be myself.
We played gin rummy, tiddledywinks,
and I always cheated. He was a wolf,
or at least was eaten by one. Sometimes,
I suspect everyone alive is dead
or pretending to be. This explains
the nature of the crepe, which dares not
rise to heaven no matter how soft
those lutes appear. His fur was worn
brown and full of faded surprises,
like the sun on a Texas birthday party.
I'm still waiting to hear back from
his lawyer on whether we've got
a case with this thing or have to keep
on living this way, if you can call it that.

A Ship in a Bottle

The past tense of me is us. As in
we rode the bed like a ship
in a bottle. A kind of nimbus coloring
the horizon. Nothing to think
but the flow of water bumping
against the box spring. Now, my bed
is covered in books my daughter
has read, is reading, hasn't read yet.
It used to be stuffies and peppermints.
A soft blanket for scary nights.
My sheets are clean. There's no one
to make them dirty. We never spent
as much time in bed as we could've.
There was always something else
to do. Hoist the sail. Batten the hatches.
We were searching for the island
we wanted to die on. But we never
found it, just glimpses. I've seen
dragons and sea serpents. Mermaids
and sirens, singing their lovely songs.
They never sing to me. Not since
you left.

Eulogy

If I can't cry for you, how can I cry
for myself? Someday, they'll find you,
lightning burned tongue, wings long pawned,
liver eaten by vultures, a ring of ashes around
your head. So much is left to say.
The cars never stop coming.
The crows argue in my chimney. No one
could hurt me so well if they didn't love me.
The hours have to be filled somehow.
When I put her to bed, my daughter says,
I love you. I'll miss you. Goodnight. Does anyone
miss you? Stumbling into the night, so cruel,
you wear sunglasses to hide your eyes.
Every day and forever.
I love you. I'll miss you. Goodbye.

You Won't Be Seeing Me Again

after a line by NOFX

The heart is finite, but the world's pain
blossoms like the rains in spring. Don't let
the crystal sniffers fool you
into throwing yourself on its thorns.
The world is always burning, and our hearts
are made of wood. It's lovely to think
otherwise. If you're very lucky, you can tamp
down the flames closest to you.

It's so tempting to say that you never loved
me, rather than that you just grew bored
of my heart itching around your door. So much
is dying, and I want to tell you about it all,
but you were so terse on the phone with me
the last time you accidentally dialed my number.
My body has changed. My ways have changed.
My heart remains the same. The me you used
to know died in the snow when you left him.
You wouldn't know me anymore, if you ever did.

Stone

All love is improvisation. When she says yes
and when she says no. When a child
asks if they can shave their head,
and you say wait until tomorrow,
until Mercury is no longer in retrograde,
until your hair has had a say. So long
I've wished to be loved. I've made
myself a stone, easy to carry with. But
so rarely do women's dresses have
pockets. Wear me on a string, then.
I can unfurl into a helpmeet. I can
soften into something fine. I think
on my feet like the best of them.
I just need somewhere to stand.

Take So Long

Will you remember the time the trap
in my old apartment caught a mouse
but didn't kill it? Tiny body breaking,
it screamed. I ran with it to the bathroom.
"Let it out the window," you said, maybe
seven or eight. I told you I had, wasn't
sure if you believed me or not. Its fur
the color of our carpet, I drowned
the thing in the toilet. Or will you remember
how I stayed? It's so hard, missing you.
So many false starts I've made to fill
the time away. When my mother
was sick, this one nurse would walk
her down the hill to meet me at the bus.
I would sneak past to go be with my
father at the Fish Shack. Once, she called
to me, "Get back here with your mother."
It was exciting, men drinking, telling jokes.
Dying slow is so dull. I couldn't wait for it
even then.

The Ghost Is Tired of Its Sheet

A cup of tea as lifemate.
A cold wind as confidante.
I never stood a chance.

Slicked back hair and shoeshine teeth.
The most beautiful woman I've ever seen.
The ghost is haunting its own wounds.
The ghost has a clipboard and a to-do list a mile long.

I miss you most when you tell me not to.
I believe everything you ever said
except goodbye.

Clutter is a life with no direction.
I keep everything as orderly as a clam.

Bipolar means I miss you when I'm happy and sad.
The ghost of the worst relationship I've ever had.
I'm not taking calls after ten anymore.
How long until you show up at my door?

That High Lonesome House

It almost snowed. So close to winter, my feet
perpetually cold. My daughter screamed awake
with a spider crawling down the wall above her bed,
she'd just gotten to sleep in spite of a nasty cough.
There's so much to do before spring. I have to find
love. I have to clean the bathroom. The kitchen. My soul.
I can sell books to pay someone. Does that make me
a class traitor or just tired? But I'm grateful
for the books, grateful for the updates on my father,
dying. Coming home to someone else's noise.
We used to roll down the ridge, trying to flush
snakes. One of them chased me up a fence one
time. My sister swears she remembers carrying
me through the snow after a seizure, but I didn't have
those until my preteens. Once, my sister called
to ask if the lake was frozen. I ran to the barbed wire
fence in my underwear and climbed up to look,
but got caught in the barbs and called to mom
to help, afraid the neighbors would hear down the hill
and look up to catch me, so I climbed out of them,
left them on the fence, and ran back to the TV.

Working from Home

You want to say something nice to Tim,
your coworker, who is dating five women,
but your brother just died, your ex-girlfriend
is slowly being revealed as a narcissist,
in hindsight, and when the shame spiral,
the panic attacks flare, you're trying not
to think about the bottles of sleeping pills,
the opiates in your bathroom. Your ex-wife
says it's PTSD. You can barely make it till 4
without mixing a drink. He messaged to say
he's worried because the one he likes made
a joke about marriage. You say communication
is what makes a relationship strong. He says
he's dumped two of them. The last time,
he was dating three, broke it off with two
in the same night and then the third dumped
him a week later. What makes her so nice?
you ask and he says they come from similar
backgrounds, she makes him laugh. Your ex
was the most charming person you've ever met.
Her attention was like a spotlight, and you got
to be a star while she shone on you. As long
as you dressed the way she wanted, didn't say
or do the things she didn't like. As long
as you pleased her, every moment, and didn't let
her grow bored. When things would finally start
to feel safe, she'd complain of it being stagnant.
When you finally felt something close to loved,
she'd say she needed space. Tim says this woman

likes him maybe too much. I'm great but not that
great, he says. You're aight, you say. Your ex
told you the kindest things anyone has ever told
you after she destroyed you one morning. You'd
driven home, shaking and crying while she chatted
on the phone about her plans for the day, and after
your emergency therapy session, you told her
your therapist said you should stick it out (but have
an exit strategy). She was shocked. Were you
thinking about breaking up? she asked. You've
forgotten all those kind things, but you'll never
forget that morning, in the hotel, your joy, your love
forever evaporating. You never really loved me,
she said the last time she called. You just wanted
to be saved, which is exactly what she wanted.
Tim bought a house and is learning how paint
works, the difference between wet and dry shades.
Your ex calls drunk saying how lonely she is.
She says stop loving me so we can be friends. No one
else could ever want you, you know. Not like that
spotlight. That's part of what she taught you in the hotel,
and every day you were together and every day
since. Your sister calls to say she's been crying
for days about your brother and you say what
I wouldn't give to be able to cry. You say my brother
died, too. Tim has been getting sloppy drunk at work
since we've been working from home. His seasonal
depression. What you wouldn't give for yours
to only happen in the winter. You drink most
days but don't make mistakes. The wisdom
of age. You don't get to see your daughter
as much now, so you're adrift. Your ex talked
about children when she was sloppy drunk.

What a shitshow that would've been, but you
would've done it. You're young, you want
to tell Tim. Life will get so much harder. But
maybe it won't, for him. He's good looking.
He's confident. She would take your arm
and walk beside you to the movie theater,
to dinner. All your life, you've just wanted
someone to love. Ever since your mother died.
What a cliché. You have so much love
to give, a friend once told you. It feels good
to talk about this stuff, Tim says. Is there anything
I can help you with? No, you say. But thank
you. Just take care of yourself.

She Died Doing What She Loved: Being Eaten by a Monkey Who Mistook Her Mr. Belvedere Costume for a Banana.

I see a face on TV, and I am angry.
I see a couple arguing on the sidewalk, and I am angry.
Squirrels chasing each other.
Birds that won't shut up.
I see children laughing in the street, and I am angry.

I see your name in my missed calls, and I am angry.
I see you talking to your friend.
I see your face and I am angry.
I can't stop thinking about all the ways you hurt me.

I lie in bed, and I am angry.
I imagine the weather, and I am angry.
I sit at my computer.
I run to the bathroom.
I order take out.
I watch bad TV.
All day, I am angry.
All day, I hate my heart for believing you.

Self-Portrait as Mostly Light 3

after a line by Michael Sikkema

At least the road to hell is paved. At least
I won't be alone there. I'm very serious
when it comes to pies and people
I won't let into my life anymore. Fool
me twice, let's get married. You're more
of a pothole than a good intention.
Light glides across my kitchen wall.
It's just somebody trying to get home.
You get so used to being lost you set
up house there. Hire a maid to dust
off your heart. Adventure awaits
if I can stop crying long enough.

You Must Believe in Spring

Fire burns from the bottom up,
when you've stacked the wood
correctly. Most mornings,
I lie awake thinking of your face,
the way you throw your head back
when you laugh, eyes closed
in explosion. Are you laughing, now?
Are you happy? When it's chilly,
I make fires with the wood I bought
to burn with you. If it's not cold
enough, I open the door. Poem drafts.
Boxes. Kindling. Gifts in every room.
You left so much in my life when
you said goodbye. A tornado
in once clear skies. Everything scattered
and broken behind. Crows
try to nest in my chimney, laughing
as they soar away.

Cathy

Was it a third or fourth date? The idea
was for you to stop at a Cuban food
truck and bring sandwiches that we'd sneak
into West Side Story. I got to the theater
early, wrote a poem about the moon
breaking my heart. The truck was closed
or too busy or something went wrong,
so you brought Burger King instead.
Grease and salt, comfortable smell; you tucked
the bag into the hood of your coat,
and I got tickets. Inside, we settled in
to wait until it was dark. We ate quickly
while Maria and Tony danced and sang.
Your eyes burned the lightest blue.
It was early yet. There was all the time
in the world.